P9-CAF-219

WITHDRAWN

The SOLDIERS' Voice

The SOLDIERS' Voice:

The Story of Ernie Pyle

by Barbara O'Connor

WITHDRAWN

 Carolrhoda Books, Inc./Minneapolis

For Bill and Dixie O'Connor

I am grateful to the many veterans of World War II and their spouses who sent me clippings and photos of Ernie Pyle; to Lt. Kenneth Barden and George Shaffer, who shared their memories of Ernie; to Bill O'Connor, Jr., for his interest in this project; to my editor, Jill Anderson; and to David Nichols, for so generously sharing his expertise.

Quotes from Ernie Pyle's columns, including "The Death of Captain Waskow," are reprinted by permission of Scripps Howard Foundation.

The letters written by Ernie Pyle that are quoted in the text are housed at the Ernie Pyle State Historical Site, in Dana, Indiana, and at Lilly Library, Indiana University at Bloomington.

Text copyright © 1996 by Barbara O'Connor

All rights reserved. International copyright secured. No part of this book may be reproduced, stored in a retrieval system, or transmitted in any form or by any means, electronic, mechanical, photocopying, recording, or otherwise, without the prior written permission of Carolrhoda Books, Inc., except for the inclusion of brief quotations in an acknowledged review.

Carolrhoda Books, Inc. c/o The Lerner Group
241 First Avenue North, Minneapolis, MN 55401

LIBRARY OF CONGRESS CATALOGING-IN-PUBLICATION DATA
O'Connor, Barbara.
   The soldiers' voice : the story of Ernie Pyle / by Barbara O'Connor.
      p.   cm.
   Includes bibliographical references and index.
   ISBN 0–87614–942–5 (lib. bdg.)
   1. Pyle, Ernie, 1900–1945—Juvenile literature. 2. War correspondents—United States—Biography—Juvenile literature. 3. World War, 1939–1945—Journalists—Juvenile literature. [1. Pyle, Ernie, 1900–1945. 2. War correspondents. 3. Journalists. 4. World War, 1939–1945.] I. Title.
PN4874.P86O28 1996
070.4'333'092—dc20
[B]   94–44283
                                                                            CIP
                                                                             AC

Manufactured in the United States of America
1 2 3 4 5 6 – JR – 01 00 99 98 97 96

Contents

Farm Boy

Ernie Pyle climbed up onto the seat of a horse-drawn plow and frowned as he looked out at the flat, dusty fields of an Indiana farm. He had spent many happy afternoons walking behind the plow, dragging his bare feet through the soft, freshly turned earth while his father urged on the three big horses. Now it was his turn to drive the plow. After all, he was nine years old, the same age his father had been when he first learned to plow.

A lot of farm boys would have been proud and excited to be plowing for the first time, but not Ernie. He would rather have been sitting on the front porch listening to his mother or Aunt Mary read stories or fishing in the creek with his dog, Shep. In fact, he would rather have been doing almost anything but driving that plow, because Ernie Pyle just plain didn't like farming. Never did and never would.

Ernie's parents, Will and Maria, had never known any-

Will and Maria Pyle with their only son, Ernest, and his dog, Shep. Ernie's pals nicknamed him "Shag" because of his shaggy mop of red hair.

thing but farming. They had both been raised on farms. It was only natural that after they were married in 1899, they moved into a rented farmhouse just outside of the little town of Dana, Indiana. There they set to work sharecropping, growing crops on land that belonged to someone else. The Pyles had to share what they grew with the owner of the land, but they managed to earn enough to live on. They were simple folks with simple needs.

Will Pyle was a good, quiet man who believed in clean living and honesty. "If he has an enemy in this whole country, I have yet to hear about it," Ernie wrote about him years later. Will Pyle wasn't one to talk much about what he liked and didn't like, but Ernie always suspected his father didn't care much for farming either. Maria was different. She loved farming and all the work that went with it. "My mother would rather drive a team of horses in the field than cook a dinner," Ernie wrote. To Maria Pyle, hard work and happiness went hand in hand.

Three-year-old Ernie poses on a rocking horse he received for Christmas.

On August 3, 1900, the Pyles' first and only child was born in the Dana farmhouse. Maria named him Ernest Taylor Pyle. To her and Will, he would always be Ernest—not Shag, as his childhood friends often called him (because of his shaggy, reddish hair) and never Ernie, as everyone else called him.

When Ernie was eighteen months old, the Pyles moved a few miles down the road to live with Maria's sister, Mary, on the family farm. Those few miles would be as far as Ernie went for quite a while. But he must have been born restless. Even as a young boy, he found himself dreaming of places far beyond the farm—places way down the gravel road to Dana and clear on over the Illinois border, places far more exciting and interesting than a farm. Maybe someday he would visit all the places in the picture postcards he collected and pasted in a scrapbook. But Ernie the dreamer rarely wandered far from home, for just the short drive into Dana could set the butterflies to fluttering in his stomach. "I was a farm boy," he wrote, "and town kids can make you feel awfully backward when you're young and a farm boy."

If the town kids were looking for someone to pick on, Ernie was surely easy prey. Besides being small and frail looking, as a boy he had a high-pitched voice that squeaked when he got excited. He had gotten into the habit of clearing his throat before he spoke—his "no-squeak insurance." There wasn't much sophistication about the scrawny, shaggy haired, squeaky voiced Ernie Pyle.

Ernie learned at an early age that farm life meant work and lots of it. There were fields to plow and fences to mend and chickens to feed. There were cows to milk (which Ernie wasn't very good at) and corn cribs to build (which he was pretty good at). Ernie was also pretty good at hunting down a good time and someone to share it with. His best friend was a boy named Thad Hooker. "We thought the world would end if we didn't see each other every day," Ernie remembered.

Ernie and Thad experienced a lot of things together, but boredom was rarely one of them. Because Ernie was small for his age, he preferred to stay away from sports. But he had a vivid imagination and a fine sense of humor, and he used both to invent games and pranks and other forms of childish fun for Thad and himself. One of their favorite games was Knights of the Round Table. With the battered lid of an old pot for a shield and a wooden pole for a spear, Sir Ernie rode his pony into battle with his loyal friend Sir Thad at his side.

When the two boys tired of that game, they ran through

the pastures and down to the little creek a mile or so from the Pyle farm. The creek was too shallow to swim in, but Ernie and Thad did the best they could. They took off their overalls and went "mud-crawling," lying down on their stomachs in the shallow water and walking on their hands along the muddy bottom. It may not have been as good as swimming, but it turned out to be a pretty good way to fish. One day when Ernie was mud-crawling, a big fish swam right into his underwear. It was the biggest fish he had ever caught, and he proudly took it home and ate it for dinner.

In 1914, when Ernie was fourteen, a little excitement came to the Pyle farm. Will Pyle bought his first car. After a lifetime of driving only wagons and plows, driving a car took Will a little getting used to. Ernie never forgot the day the three Pyles climbed into their new car for an outing into Dana. When they got home, Ernie and Maria got out and watched Will drive into the wagon shed, where he kept the car. A few seconds later, the door on the opposite side of the shed flew open and the wagon leaped out, crashing down a hill and into a gravel pit below. Another time, Will oiled the squeaking brakes of his car and drove into town, over the curb, and right through the window of a dry-goods store. Eventually, though, he got the hang of driving enough to teach Ernie.

When Ernie was sixteen, Will bought him a car of his own: a Model T Ford Roadster. Ernie and Thad now felt an independence they had never known before. They had gotten to the "girl stage," so the two young men would climb into Ernie's car with their dates and head off for the

Ernie at sixteen

local skating rink. A car, a girl, and a corncob pipe had a way of making the puniest farm boy feel like a big-city man.

One summer Ernie got a chance to go to the Indianapolis 500, one of the best-known car races in the United States, and he came home with a new dream. He wanted to be a race car driver and live a life of action, excitement, and daring. A race car driver was a hero, and Ernie wanted to be a hero too.

But driving cars wasn't the only way Ernie saw to get some glory. When the United States entered World War I by declaring war against Germany on April 6, 1917, young men across the country eagerly enlisted in the military. The men of Dana were no exception. To Ernie it seemed as if plain old ordinary farm boys turned into heroes overnight. Ernie longed to join them, but his parents insisted that he finish high school first. So he watched his friends and neighbors go off to war, to places he could only dream about. How lucky they were, he thought, to leave the dull routines of Dana, Indiana, for a new adventure in a far-off place.

When his buddy Thad entered the army, Ernie again begged his parents to let him go. How could he possibly stay home and milk cows while Thad was off fighting for his country? But Will and Maria stood firm. Ernest was staying right where he was. He was going to finish high school, and that was that.

In the spring of 1918, Ernie attended his high school graduation ceremony. Sitting on stage with his classmates, waiting to receive his diploma, Ernie should have felt proud and happy. But when he looked at the places where his friend Thad and the other enlistees would have sat and saw the empty, flag-draped chairs, Ernie felt ashamed that he wasn't in the army too.

A few weeks after graduation, Ernie rushed over to Peoria, Illinois, and enlisted in the Naval Reserves. After basic training in nearby Champaign, Illinois, Ernie prepared to move on to another training station. He could hardly wait. If he couldn't be a race car driver, he could at least be a soldier. But fate would not have it. On November 11, 1918, shortly before he was to begin his training, an armistice was signed, ending the war. While the world rejoiced, a disappointed young Ernie Pyle returned to the farm.

CHAPTER 2

Not Just Pictures on a Postcard

Less than a year after his return home, in the fall of 1919, Ernie was once again packing his suitcases and kissing his mother good-bye. This time he was off to Bloomington, Indiana, for his first year at Indiana University. Bloomington was only sixty miles away, but to a bashful nineteen-year-old with little experience beyond the chicken yard, it was another world. Ernie's vision of becoming a race car driver had dimmed, but a fast car could still turn his head quicker than a pretty girl. In one of his first letters home, he told Will, Maria, and Aunt Mary all about the "big fine machines down here."

Though shy, Ernie had a natural, easygoing manner and a knack for making friends. Classes had not even started when Ernie met Paige Cavanaugh, a kindred spirit who would become Ernie's lifelong friend. Like Ernie, Paige was an Indiana farm boy anxious to leave home for bigger things. Unlike Ernie, Paige had fought in the war.

Ernie was drawn to him right away, feeling at home with his country manner, yet awed and envious of his wartime adventures. "He thought the war was a great experience for me," Paige recalled years later, "and he regretted that he'd not been able to be a part of it—the risk, the romance, the adventure of it, perhaps." Ernie just couldn't quite shake the feeling that he had missed something by not joining his old pal Thad in the war.

Ernie quickly settled into campus life, sipping Cokes with friends at the local soda fountain. At first he didn't much care what courses he took, since he wasn't sure yet what career he wanted to pursue. About all he was sure of was that he didn't want to be stuck in one place, tied down to a routine with no chance for a change of scenery—like a farmer. Paige suggested that Ernie sign up to major in journalism. "At least you don't have to add and subtract," he told Ernie. That sounded good to Ernie. But journalism wasn't available to freshmen, so Ernie decided to major in economics instead.

During his first year of college, Ernie wrote home faithfully once a week. So his folks wouldn't think he'd taken on any big-city airs, he always remembered to ask about the farm. "How are your lambs and chickens getting along?" he asked his parents. "Glad your hogs did so well," he wrote to Aunt Mary.

The following year, 1920, Ernie decided to take Paige's advice and enroll in a journalism class. As it turned out, Ernie had a natural talent for newspaper writing. By the second semester of his sophomore year, he had joined the staff of the college newspaper, the *Indiana Daily Student*.

Ernie enjoyed journalism, but he still dreamed of travel and adventure. The summer he turned twenty-one, he finally got a chance to see a little more of the world. Still in the Naval Reserves, he got to go on a three-week training cruise. The ship, the *Wilmette,* sailed from Chicago up Lake Michigan and across Lake Superior to Duluth, Minnesota. It was the farthest from home Ernie had ever been. Unfortunately, he spent most of the cruise cooking in the galley (the ship's kitchen). Instead of seeing the world, about all Ernie saw was a greasy frying pan and a hot stove.

At the beginning of his junior year, in 1921, Ernie was made city editor of the *Student.* In November, the *Student* published a series of articles describing the burial of the Unknown Soldier in Arlington National Cemetery, in Virginia. Ernie was deeply moved by these articles. He began to realize that there could be more to newspaper writing than just reporting the news. For the first time, Ernie began to think more about a career in journalism.

Besides his position as city editor of the *Student,* Ernie worked on the staff of the student yearbook, the *Arbutus.* Known as a likeable guy in big, sloppy clothes, Ernie was making friends and having fun, but there were times he felt unhappy for no particular reason. Since he wasn't very good at hiding his feelings, his friends usually knew when he was down in the dumps. "I remember him many times as a sad little guy," Paige would later recall.

But there was one person who could always snap Ernie out of a blue mood—a pretty redhead named Harriett Davidson. Ernie had plenty to do attending classes, studying, working on the yearbook, and writing for the *Student,* but he managed to squeeze in some time to fall in love. Harriett was a good-natured young woman who enjoyed Ernie's boyish humor. In a letter home that year, Ernie wrote, "I took my girl to the dance and there was such a big bunch of fellows there without dates that I sold two dances for a quarter apiece. . . . If I had been her I expect I would have gotten mad, but she didn't."

In March 1922, when Ernie was twenty-one, another chance to travel came his way. The university baseball team had been invited to play in Japan. "I've just got to go!" Ernie told Paige. He got permission from the dean of the university, borrowed two hundred dollars, and set out with three friends for Seattle, Washington. There, Ernie and his friends managed to get jobs on the *Keystone State,* the steamship that was carrying the baseball team to Japan.

While on board, Ernie mailed an article back to the *Student* describing his experiences on the voyage, which included getting seasick and sailing through a terrible storm. He signed the article "Ernest T. Pyle." It was his first by-line (an author's name printed with an article).

At last Ernie was able to see real places, not just pictures on a postcard. He was having so much fun he didn't care when he found out his job would require him to stay with the ship instead of touring with the baseball team. But before returning to Bloomington, he saw the Japanese port cities of Yokohama, Tokyo, and Kobe, as well as parts of China and the Philippines.

In the fall of 1922, Ernie began his senior year at the

THE INDIANA DAILY STUDENT

"O, A Sailor's Life Is The Life For Me," Says Our Ernie Pyle

Student Scribe Hops Bells At Great Rate on Keystone State —Benham Tends Bar.

Big Liner Takes On Chinese Crew at Hong Kong—Nothing To Do But Count Waves.

(Ernest T. Pyle, '23)

Amid the hurried farewells of those on board and the shouts of God-speed from those on the dock, the huge liner Keystone State, of the Admiral line, slipped away from the wharves at Smith Cove, Seattle at 11:20 a. m. Saturday, April 1, and steered out into Puget Sound on the first lap of her voyage to Far Eastern shores.

And aboard her were 13 sturdy baseball warriors of Indiana University, Coach and Mrs. Levis, Dean and Mrs. Edmondson and the four soldiers of fortune, working their way to the Orient. The ship's orchestra played on deck un+' '' the pr ngers vere safe¹ ' 's

> **AT LAST! CRIMSON WINS.**
> Osaka, Japan, May 7 (Delayed) —Indiana University's baseball team won its first game on foreign soil here today by defeating the Osaka Stars 9-4.

four days had elapsed everyone was feeling fine.

Pass Near Alaskan Coasts.

As the ship was taking the shorter northern route, we passed within a short distance of the Alaskan coast about the fourth day out, and it is said that had the days been clear, the passengers would have been able to see the Aleutian Islands. It was terribly cold up there, with snow and sleet flying and the wind blowing a gale. The boys were slightly handicapped in their battle for perfect J ᵔalth by the fact that their cabins   ᵔᵔted on the lower deck fo·   ᵔ r·   ' ro¹'

The article Ernie wrote about his trip to Japan gives a glimpse of the lively writing style he would become known for.

university. He had done a lot in the three years since leaving Dana, but now he experienced something new: a broken heart. His girlfriend, Harriett, left him to be with someone else. Ernie had always been a little moody, but now he was devastated. Harriett had not only broken his heart, but she had hurt his pride.

While Ernie was trying to get over Harriett, he got an offer to become a reporter for the *La Porte Herald,* the newspaper of La Porte, Indiana. He was pretty good at newspaper reporting, and here was a chance to get paid for it. He figured he'd be foolish not to try it. It didn't matter to him that he'd have to quit school a few months short of graduating. School had never been important to him before, and now that Harriett had left him, he saw no reason to stay in Bloomington. Despite his parents objections, Ernie took the job.

When Ernie showed up at the *La Porte Herald* office in January 1923, he was lovesick and inexperienced, but eager to learn more about the newspaper business. Charles Beal, the editor of the *Herald,* didn't think much of him, but the paper needed a reporter. Ernie would have to do.

Ernie moved into the YMCA, then got right to work covering stories at the local police station, the courthouse, and city hall. Although the *La Porte Herald* was a small newspaper in a small city, it was a big opportunity for Ernie to learn the ropes of newspaper reporting.

But just a few months after Ernie started his new job, an even bigger opportunity came his way. The Scripps Howard newspaper chain was looking for a reporter for one of its newspapers, the *Washington Daily News,* in Washington, D.C. Ernie had been recommended by a former classmate from the university. When the *Daily News* offered him the job in May 1923, Ernie jumped at the chance.

Just as he had been eager to leave the farm in Dana, now he wasted no time in saying good-bye to the cornfields of the Midwest and heading for the nation's capital. For an aspiring young journalist, Washington, D.C., was the place to be. It was the hub of politics and the home of some of the finest newspapers in the country. Washington was also a beautiful city, with its wide, tree-lined streets and neat, clean buildings. Nearly every block featured something interesting to see, from the White House to the Washington Monument to the Potomac River.

Walking to work for the first time, Ernie felt as if he were "walking with the world ahead of [him]." The editor of the *Daily News* walked with him, and as Ernie took in the sights, the editor offered some friendly advice. "You'll probably like Washington," he said to Ernie. "But let me warn you. Don't stay here too long. It's a nice, easygoing city, and people get in a rut, and if you stay till you get to liking it too well, you'll never leave."

To an Indiana farm boy who had long since vowed not to get in a rut, that was good advice.

CHAPTER
3

Full of Beans and Energy

The office of the *Washington Daily News,* just a few blocks from the White House, was small, cluttered, and noisy. Shabby secondhand desks stood end to end, covered with papers and books. Wads of crumpled paper littered the floor. Letters, notices, and memos covered the walls. Typewriters clattered, telephones rang, and busy reporters scurried in and out, trying to get their stories finished in time to be printed. Ernie was looking for action, and he had certainly found it here. He was eager to roll up his shirt sleeves and get right to work.

Those busy days of 1923 were happy times for Ernie. He had little to worry about and a lot to do, see, and learn. At first he was a reporter, but when he showed a talent for writing headlines and reading copy, he was given a job as copy editor. Although Ernie preferred the freedom and variety of reporting to sitting at a desk all day, he wasn't about to argue. If his boss wanted him to write headlines,

Ernie (left) said of the *Washington Daily News* staff (including his friend Lee Miller, center): "We didn't make much money, but we had a lot of fun."

he would write headlines. He was at his desk each day at seven o'clock sharp, elbow to elbow with the other writers and editors on the staff.

As always, Ernie's friendly manner and sense of humor made him popular with the newspaper staff from the start. Lee Miller, a fellow Indiana native, became an especially good friend. Years later Lee would write a biography of Ernie in which he described the *Daily News* staff as "full of beans and energy."

That was certainly true of Ernie. Lee always remembered how everyone in the office insisted that they could not start their day without hearing one of Ernie's famous belches, which he could usually deliver on demand (although he always claimed he needed to eat an apple first). With that morning ritual over, Ernie, Lee, and the rest of the staff got down to work. The day was a rush of activity until five o'clock, when the newspaper was ready to go to press. Then Ernie and the others pushed their desks together and got down to the less serious business of playing cards, which usually lasted well into the night.

A good night's rest wasn't nearly as important to Ernie as good conversation, hearty laughter, and the camaraderie of close friends. He also enjoyed a hefty swig of bootleg (illegal) gin from a Mason jar passed around the poker table. Prohibition, a ban on the manufacture and sale of alcohol, had been in effect for nearly four years, but the neighborhood bootlegger was only a phone call away.

By the fall of 1924, Ernie's broken heart was well mended. That was fortunate, because another young woman was about to steal it away from him. Her name was Geraldine Siebolds, Jerry for short. A clerk for the Civil Service Commission, Jerry was smart, pretty, and loved a good time. Washington had its share of handsome young men to call on her. But when she met funny little Ernie Pyle in his old, woolen stocking cap and plaid lumberjack shirt, she couldn't resist his bashful smile and wry humor.

Ernie and Jerry had a lot in common, especially their carefree attitudes. Doing interesting things and having fun were at the top of their lists of important things in life. Making money and following the rules of society were way down at the bottom.

The following year, 1925, Ernie asked Jerry to marry him, then waited nervously for her to make up her mind. Jerry loved Ernie, but she wasn't so sure marriage was for her. She was an independent woman who was content to spend time alone, reading or writing poetry. Marriage seemed a little too conventional for her. But Ernie didn't want to upset his parents by living with Jerry without being married.

Finally she agreed to marriage on one condition: that they keep it a secret from everyone except their families. Jerry had a reputation as a nonconformist, and she intended to keep it. That was fine with Ernie. On July 7, they crossed the Potomac River into Alexandria, Virginia, and were married by a justice of the peace. (For many years, they continued to insist they weren't married and Jerry refused to wear a wedding ring.)

Soon Ernie and Jerry were happily settled in an apartment on Connecticut Avenue. They had no use for furniture or neatly decorated rooms. A couple of army cots and a grill for cooking were home sweet home to them. Neither one of them cared much for domestic chores either. Their idea of housekeeping was usually just sweeping the tobacco off the floor (they both rolled their own cigarettes) and throwing out the empty bottles that accumulated on the windowsills.

By 1926, when Ernie was nearly twenty-six years old, he had tired of his job at the *News.* Sitting at a desk day after day was making him itch to get out and wander a bit. When he suggested to Jerry that they quit their jobs, buy a car, and hit the road, she thought it was a fine idea.

That June, Ernie strapped sleeping bags and some camping equipment to the fender of his new Model T, said good-bye to his buddies at the *Daily News,* and headed south with Jerry sitting contentedly beside him. For as long as he could remember, he'd had a craving to see new places, to follow any old road to any old place.

In June 1926, Ernie and Jerry strapped their belongings onto their Model T, donned traveling clothes, and hit the road.

Now that he finally had a chance to do it, he was determined to make the most of it. He drove nine thousand miles in ten weeks.

First they traveled across the South, through Texas, and clear out to Los Angeles. There they stopped for a week to visit Ernie's old college friend Paige. From there, they drove up the coast of California to Oregon, across the northern states, and then to Dana for a visit with Ernie's parents.

In August 1926, they arrived in New York City "in a downpouring rain, on two cylinders, with knots as big as teakettles on all four tires, and had to sell the precious thing for a mere hundred and fifty dollars in order to get something to eat." With empty wallets and no car, the Pyles had little choice but to stay put for a while.

Almost immediately, Ernie knew New York was not his kind of city. He hated the "frightening and unnatural skyscrapers," the dirty rivers, and the crowds of people rushing about. The basement apartment he and Jerry moved into was dingy, stuffy, and rat infested. Even finding a job, first at the *New York Evening World* and then at the *New York Post,* didn't improve his opinion of the city.

Ernie's happiest day in New York was the day Lee Miller called from Washington asking him to come back to the *Daily News.* Lee had been promoted to managing editor, and he wanted Ernie on his staff as telegraph editor (the person who edited news stories that had been transmitted by telegraph).

On Saturday, December 24, 1927, Ernie and Jerry were back in Washington. Ernie couldn't have gotten a better Christmas present. Bright and early Monday morning, he was back at the cluttered office, ready to get to work. After a few months, however, Ernie's familiar restlessness returned. He just had to find something to do that would get him out from behind his desk. Finally Ernie had an idea: a newspaper column about aviators.

In 1928 the world of aviation was still new. It had been only one year since Charles Lindbergh had made the first solo flight across the Atlantic Ocean. It would be another four years before Amelia Earhart would be the first woman to do the same. Airmail service was just three years old, and commercial passenger service was just beginning. Many of the fliers had been trained in World War I and were now making a living any way they could—from mail delivery service to aerial photography.

To Ernie, aviators were heroes, men of action like the race car drivers he had idolized as a boy. He wanted so much to write about them, he offered to do it in addition to his copyediting job. The *Daily News* agreed to let Ernie try it. On March 26, 1928, Ernie Pyle's first column appeared in the pages of the *News*—the first daily aviation column in the United States.

CHAPTER

4

Man-Killing Work

Ernie kept his end of the bargain and continued his editing job. But the minute his work was done, he rushed from the office to a nearby airport, where he spent the rest of the day just hanging around, talking to pilots, asking questions, listening to stories. Many of the pilots Ernie talked to had bought old military airplanes retired from the war. Lacking the high-tech equipment of modern aircraft, the little planes with their tiny, open cockpits were not always reliable. A routine flight could easily turn into a daring adventure. Pilots in 1928 needed skill, courage, and a good parachute.

Within a few months, Ernie was a familiar face at airports and military air stations all around Washington. Amelia Earhart once said, "Not to know Ernie Pyle is to admit that you yourself are unknown in aviation."

The aviators liked talking to Ernie, and he liked listening. Whenever anything newsworthy happened, the pilots made sure their pal Ernie got the scoop first. Once, one of the first American airmail pilots, Verne Treat, had to parachute out of his airplane into the snowy night. After landing safely, he headed for the nearest telephone to make two calls: the first to the postal service, the second to Ernie Pyle.

Before long, the Pyle apartment became a popular gathering place for pilots and their families. They dropped in at all hours of the day and night. If the telephone wasn't ringing, the doorbell was. Oftentimes, Ernie was just plain tuckered out at the end of the day, but he never turned anyone away. When everyone had finally left, Ernie would write his aviation column and fall into bed exhausted.

Ernie never became a pilot, but he logged over 100,000 miles as a passenger during his four years as an aviation columnist.

Working two jobs, drinking too much, and sleeping too little soon began to take its toll on Ernie. In June 1928, Paige Cavanaugh came to visit. The two friends hadn't seen each other in two years, and Paige could see the effects of Ernie's hard work right away. "He looked like an old man," Paige recalled. Ernie was only twenty-seven.

As the aviation column gained popularity, Ernie's boss at the *Daily News* agreed to find a new telegraph editor and let him devote all of his time to the column. No longer tied down to office hours and paperwork, Ernie had found his ideal job. He roamed around on his own schedule, collecting stories, and in the evening he still had the energy to entertain his friends. Ernie spent the next four years as aviation editor, at first exclusively for the *Daily News,* then for the more than twenty newspapers in the Scripps Howard chain.

Ernie loved his job, his wife, and his friends, but just as in his college days, he sometimes found himself feeling sad. He couldn't quite put his finger on exactly why. Paige joked, "I think he was troubled because he had nothing to complain about." Sometimes he just had a case of "the winter depressions," as he called it. He hated cold weather and got "the miseries from going around all huddled up." But Ernie was probably feeling twinges of his old unrest too. He had been back in Washington for years now, and his urge to keep moving must have left him unsatisfied, bored, and sometimes downright depressed.

In 1932 Ernie was offered the position of managing editor at the *Daily News.* (His friend Lee had changed to

Ernie (left) with some pilot friends

a different position at Scripps Howard.) Now Ernie faced one of the hardest decisions he had ever had to make. He loved writing the aviation column and the independence that went with it. He hated the prospect of sitting in an office all day, and he hated the schedules and responsibilities of a managing editor. But the United States was in the middle of the Great Depression, a period when times were hard and thousands of Americans were unemployed. The job of managing editor was a secure, well-paid position. Ernie knew he would be foolish not to take it.

Ernie was thirty-two years old when he announced to a shocked and disappointed aviation community that he was quitting the column. The pilots would miss him. During a farewell ceremony for Ernie at Washington-Hoover Airport, Amelia Earhart presented him with a beautiful watch. (He was wearing that watch the day he died.)

For the next three years, Ernie's typewriter sat in a corner gathering dust while Ernie spent his days handling the everyday problems of running a newspaper. In a letter to a friend, Ernie wrote, "I am still managing editor, but it is not a job that I like. It is hard and fatiguing work, and I get no chance to do any writing. I think that is where my greatest satisfaction lies—in writing—in expressing my feelings in print, and I don't get a chance to do it now. Maybe things will change later."

Oddly, his remedy for restlessness came out of a bad case of the flu. It was December 1934, and he was so tired and worn out that he just couldn't seem to get well. When his doctor suggested a vacation in a warmer climate, Ernie took his advice.

So once again, Ernie and Jerry hit the road. They ran into one problem though. They couldn't find any warm weather! They went south to Alabama, where it was four degrees. They went west to Arizona, where it was cool and rainy. They went farther west to Los Angeles. Still no sunny weather. Finally they gave up and decided to take a cruise from Los Angeles to Philadelphia. It wasn't warm, but at least Ernie could rest.

The cruise took three weeks. Ernie said he wished it had taken three years. There was no routine to the day. They could do whatever they wanted. And there were lots of interesting people to talk to. Ernie was in heaven. He returned to work healthy and relaxed.

Shortly afterward, in April 1935, he filled in for a vacationing columnist by writing eleven articles about his trip. The articles were a big hit with readers.

Back at his typewriter, Ernie felt like his old self again. This was where he belonged. This was what he loved. He would never be happy as managing editor. He wanted to write, and he wanted to travel. So he came up with a plan in which he could do both. He wanted to be a roving reporter, traveling to big cities and small towns across the country, writing about people, places, events—anything that interested him. Hopefully these things would interest his readers too.

Ernie presented his idea and nearly jumped for joy when his boss agreed to let him try it. In a letter to a friend, Ernie wrote, "I've had a good stroke of luck. I've finally been transferred from this man-killing job I've been on for three years. . . . I will go where I please and write what I please. It's just the kind of job I've always wanted and I hope I can make a go of it."

On August 2, 1935, the day before Ernie's thirty-fifth birthday, he and Jerry set off down the road to anyplace, just where Ernie had always wanted to go.

CHAPTER
5

Anyplace, U.S.A.

Ernie posed proudly next to the Utah state line while Jerry took his picture. This was a special occasion, and Ernie wanted a photograph to remember it by. It was the fall of 1936, and he had just crossed the border from Colorado into Utah. Now it was official. He had traveled through every state in the United States (except Alaska and Hawaii, which didn't become states until 1959).

It had been over a year since Ernie had set off on the road to anyplace. He had driven over 29,000 miles. "My arms never get tired, even on rough roads," he wrote. "But being a skinny fellow, I do get to hurting where I sit down, and I think I'll have to get an air cushion to sit on." Ernie liked to brag that in all those miles, he had just one flat tire, ran out of gas only twice, and never forgot anything in a hotel room except a toothbrush.

Right from the start, Ernie proved he had a real nose for sniffing out good stories. He loved the oddball character,

Ernie poses at the Utah border. When asked why he traveled, Ernie joked, "You don't have to make your own beds. You don't have to buy coal. You can make friends and go on before they find out how dull you are. You don't have to get up at four A.M. and milk the cows."

and if he couldn't find one himself, he would drop in at the local police station or doctor's office and ask who the most interesting person in town was.

Ernie was proud of the fact that not one person ever refused to talk to him. He had a way about him that made folks want to pull up a chair and chat. Except for jotting down a name or two now and then, he rarely took notes. He just listened. Then he told their stories in a casual, folksy way that made readers feel like he was right there on the front porch with them.

In those 29,000 miles, Ernie managed to find quite a few interesting people. There was Ellis Edmunds, from Newport News, Virginia, a railroad engineer who played tunes with his locomotive whistle. There was Mizzoo Townsend, the champion poker player of Pocatello, Idaho. And there was Rudy Hale and his wife, who caught rattlesnakes for a living near Yuma, Arizona.

In the rare case that Ernie couldn't find an amusing character to write about, he didn't worry. Ernie had a knack for making an interesting story out of just about anything. Once he wrote about the two hundred eighty-four dead grasshoppers that were stuck in his radiator in South Dakota. Another time he described how the artist Gutzon Borglum was carving the presidents' faces on Mount Rushmore. And from Baudette, Minnesota, he told about "the biggest and handsomest cobweb between here and Minneapolis."

Ernie tried not to write about anything too serious. After all, in 1935 the Depression was in full swing. Ernie thought most folks had enough to worry about without having to read about politics or economics. He was pretty sure they'd much rather travel along with him. And travel they did. They toured a soap factory in Cincinnati, Ohio, visited a log schoolhouse in Rogersville, Tennessee, and stayed on a ranch in the Arizona desert. They even went to Dana to meet Will and Maria Pyle and to Orlando, Florida, to visit Ernie's childhood buddy Thad Hooker.

Before long, Ernie began to receive letters from readers all over the country. They told him about places or people they thought he might like to write about. Ernie soon had so many ideas that he started to file them by state in a little wooden box he kept in his car.

Working his way through that file box led Ernie from coast to coast and nearly everywhere in between. Readers who rarely traveled farther than their own front gates got a glimpse of America through Ernie's eyes. He told them that Boston was the "easiest city in America to get

In Hollywood, California, Ernie stops in to chat with child actress Shirley Temple (left) and her stand-in.

lost in." He described Kansas during a drought as "the saddest land I have ever seen." And he must have insulted a few people in Eastport, Maine, when he wrote that their city smelled like sardines.

Of all the places Ernie visited, he had a special fondness for the Southwest. He expressed his affection for New Mexico when he wrote, "Boston for Beans, Seattle for rain, San Francisco for bridges, and Santa Fe for long, far looks at what God made."

Ernie also liked to write about funny things that happened to him on his travels so readers would feel as if they knew him personally. His comical adventures often turned into his most popular columns (like the time the zipper on his pants got stuck and he had to fix it with a hammer!).

His health was also a popular subject. Prone to frequent colds, Ernie joked that he was cursed with "Puny Pyle's Perpetual Pains." Too much drinking and too many roadside meals didn't help. "I claim to have been sick in more hotel rooms than any man on earth," he once said.

Soon people across the country were waiting anxiously for the newspaper to arrive so they could find out what Ernie Pyle was up to. At first most newspapers printed his columns only occasionally. But as his popularity grew, his pieces began to appear daily. A hero worshipper himself, suddenly Ernie was a hero in his own right—seeing the world, untied to home, job, and responsibility in a way his readers could never be.

As the Pyles puttered along from town to town, life was simple and home was wherever their Ford coupe took them. Ernie didn't need a thing in the world but a tank of gas and a typewriter. Jerry was the perfect traveling companion. She had no problem living out of suitcases, grabbing quick meals at diners, or napping in the car. While Ernie was out chatting with gold miners and bear trappers, Jerry would sit in the car or back at the hotel room, reading, writing poetry, or working crossword puzzles. She liked her privacy and didn't mind a bit that in his columns Ernie referred to her only as "That Girl who rides with me."

Ernie was required to send six columns a week back to Washington, where they were distributed to twenty-four Scripps Howard newspapers around the country. His habit was to spend several days collecting material before setting up his typewriter in a hotel room to write. He counted on "That Girl" to read his work, provide praise and criticism, and help him retype the columns.

Even with a talent for finding good stories, Ernie sometimes found himself struggling to get his six columns to

Washington each week. There were times when he thought he'd "rather dig potatoes for a living." To make matters worse, his friends teased him about getting paid just to take a vacation. "There are only a few roving reporters in the world," Ernie responded irritably. "My friends think it is an easy job. . . . They don't know what it is to drive and dig up information all day long, and then work till midnight writing it. One story a day sounds as easy as falling off a log. Try it sometime."

When Ernie got down in the dumps, he could feel awfully insecure about his writing. "I feel that my stuff at its very best is only just barely good enough," he complained to his friend Lee. That made finishing his six columns a week even tougher. Often Jerry was good at boosting Ernie's ego and helping him feel better again. But there were times when she, too, was depressed and moody. The two of them often tried to cure their blues by drinking too much.

Ernie was almost thirty-seven years old in the spring of 1937 when Scripps Howard asked him to go to Alaska for three months to write about the people of that remote and unfamiliar territory. Ernie and Jerry agreed that it would be best for her to stay in Washington rather than rough it in the cold Alaska wilderness. They kissed good-bye at the train station in Toledo, Ohio. Things would never be the same for Ernie and Jerry after that.

On her own for the first time in years, Jerry was lonely and increasingly depressed. Her drinking got worse, and she became dependent on prescription drugs. By the time Ernie returned from Alaska in August, Jerry was in no

In Alaska, Ernie tries his hand at panning for gold. He didn't strike it rich as a gold rusher, but he had as a journalist.

condition to hit the road with him like before. For the next two years, Ernie continued to travel, sometimes with Jerry but most often alone. As Jerry's mental and physical health declined, Ernie felt sad, confused, and helpless. The only thing he knew to do was keep on driving.

CHAPTER 6

A World at War

While Ernie had been bumping along the dusty back roads of America in the 1930s, some important events had been taking place on the other side of the world. Adolf Hitler, chancellor of Germany and leader of the German National Socialist (Nazi) party, was gearing up to make his country the most powerful in Europe. Part of the Nazis' plan was to rid Germany of all people of Jewish heritage, and the Nazis began to take away their jobs and property. Hundreds of thousands of Jews were fleeing Germany as persecution by the Nazis increased.

Ernie felt far removed from the trouble in Europe. He knew there was talk of war, but he wasn't interested in writing about it. He knew that one of the keys to his success was the light subject matter of his column. So while Hitler's army was invading Austria in March of 1938, Ernie was writing about eating chile con carne with a couple who lived in a cave in Death Valley, California.

And when Hitler occupied Czechoslovakia a year later, Ernie was writing about hookworms in Elba, Alabama.

When rumors turned to reality and Great Britain and France declared war against Germany on September 3, 1939, Ernie kept moving. Besides the Scripps Howard newspapers, his column now appeared in eight more papers from California to Florida. He had been in every state in the United States at least three times. He had "stayed in more than eight hundred hotels, [had] crossed the continent exactly twenty times, flown on sixty-six different airplanes, ridden on twenty-nine different boats, walked two hundred miles, and put out approximately twenty-five hundred dollars in tips." For a boy who had longed to travel farther than the dusty road to Dana, Ernie hadn't done too badly.

But after four years on the road, restlessness was tugging at him once again. Sure, he was moving from place to place. But he was still in a rut. His traveling life had a routine to it that had begun to bother him. And with the whole country talking of little else but the war in Europe and the possibility of the United States joining in, he was starting to get bored writing "silly dull columns."

As Ernie's spirits sagged, so did his health. When he finally took a break to visit a doctor, he was diagnosed with low blood pressure, anemia, stomach spasms (caused by his nervousness), and exhaustion. He was only thirty-nine years old, but he felt much older. "The way I feel now," he wrote a friend, "I'm only good for another year of column writing."

To add to his worries, Jerry's mental health continued

to worsen. She traveled with Ernie from time to time, but she often spent days alone in a hotel room, drinking too much and eating too little. She would be happy and animated one minute, depressed and withdrawn the next.

During the summer of 1940, the Pyles bought some land in Albuquerque, New Mexico, and began to build a house. Ernie hoped the new house would keep Jerry occupied and help lift her spirits. In the meantime, the war in Europe continued. Hitler's army had invaded Norway and continued through Denmark and Holland into Belgium. In July, Hitler bombed England.

Ernie and Jerry share a quiet moment at their new home in Albuquerque. Since he began writing his travel column, Ernie claimed he had worn out two cars, five sets of tires, three typewriters, and "pretty soon [was] going to have to have a new pair of shoes."

Finally Ernie decided he was ready to write about the war. For him, writing about something meant being right there in the middle of it, and the war would be no exception. When the Germans began bombing London, Ernie suggested to his boss at Scripps Howard that he go there to write about what was happening. Ernie "damn near fell out of [his] chair" when his boss agreed.

It had been twenty-two years since Ernie had watched with envy as Thad Hooker went off to war. Now, at the age of forty, it was his turn at last. True, he was going to war as a reporter rather than a heroic young soldier, but at least he was going. Ernie was excited about his new assignment, but there were also times he wished he had never thought of the idea. "I am scared half to death [to be so close to the fighting]," he wrote to a friend, "and Jerry is badly upset and really grieving."

Ernie left for London on November 16, 1940. Seven days later, he wrote to Jerry from on board his ship, "I keep wishing I were in New Mexico with nothing to do instead of on a boat with something to do."

When he arrived in London on December 9, he discovered for the first time what it was like to be in a war-torn city. Night after night, German planes dropped bombs. Ernie was there to see it, hear it, feel it, and write about it. He was deeply affected by the experience. Unlike his humorous, lighthearted columns about life on the road in America, his London columns took on a much more serious tone. "You could feel the shake from the guns," he wrote. "You could hear the boom, crump, crump, crump of heavy bombs at their work of tearing buildings apart."

After a night of heavy bombing, Ernie stood on the balcony of his hotel room and looked out at the city. Later, he wrote about what he saw: "This old, old city—even though I must bite my tongue in shame for saying it—was the most beautiful sight I have ever seen. It was a night when London was ringed and stabbed with fire."

Ernie's columns from London were a big hit at home.

Ernie on a London rooftop (inset). His descriptions of the bombing of London attracted many new readers.

Fifteen more newspapers began printing his column. Even Eleanor Roosevelt was a devoted reader. Ernie wasn't doing anything different from what he had been doing before. He was just describing what he saw. The difference was that now Ernie was seeing a war.

On March 3, 1941, three months after Ernie had arrived in London, he got the sad news that his mother had died of cancer. Ernie felt grief and a touch of guilt that his work had kept him away from home for such long periods of time. During the years since Ernie had left Dana, Will and Maria had received many letters but few visits from their only son.

After learning of his mother's death, Ernie expressed his feelings in writing. In a column he called "Pictures of a Mother's Lifetime," he reminisced about his childhood and some of the happy memories he had of his mother and life on the farm. In the deeply moving piece "Good-bye, Mother," Ernie described his first and only visit to his mother's grave. "As I stood there it seemed to me that she and I were all alone in the world and I could speak to her," he wrote.

When Ernie returned to the United States in late March, he was anxious for a rest and some time alone with Jerry in their new home in Albuquerque. But he knew he couldn't rest for long. Nearly three million readers expected to read Ernie Pyle with their morning coffee. He couldn't risk taking more than a short break.

As it turned out, he could neither rest nor write. His column had become so popular that he was practically a celebrity. Instead of the peace and quiet he had hoped for, his home was chaotic. Friends stopped in to visit nearly every day. Tourists drove by his house hoping to see him. "I've practically become a goldfish," Ernie complained to Lee. "If I weren't afraid of the future, I'd quit this job and raise cactus for a living." Finally Ernie checked into a hotel so he could write in peace.

After a brief stay in Albuquerque, Ernie bought a new Pontiac convertible and headed for El Paso. For the next few months, he traveled, sometimes with Jerry but usually alone. Jerry still rode an emotional roller coaster, and being with her was often difficult. Ernie knew his long absences were hard on her, but he wrote travel columns for a living. Writing travel columns meant he had to travel. He supposed he could have quit and returned to "a settled life of office hours and drudgery," he told her, but he knew himself well enough to admit that he would have been "wild within six months, which would destroy [them] both."

Exhausted from his work and frustrated by Jerry's condition, Ernie had a bad case of nervousness. "If a mouse squeaks I'll jump clear out of my skin and right out the window," he wrote to Paige. When Jerry tried to commit suicide in the summer of 1941, Ernie took her to a doctor in Denver, hoping to find an answer to her problems. The doctor could find nothing physically wrong with her. But Ernie knew that she would never be the same happy woman he had married. "My old life, I feel sure, is gone," he admitted sadly in a letter to Lee. "But it is a hard thing to abandon forever a companionship that was as close as ours was for fifteen years."

That August, Ernie made a difficult decision. He wanted to try to help Jerry, and he knew he couldn't do it if he was working. Writing a daily column required all of his time and attention. He explained his situation to Scripps Howard and offered to resign. Deac Parker, the editor-in-chief, thought so much of Ernie that he told him to take a three-month leave of absence and insisted that Ernie continue to earn his full salary. But Ernie wrote to Deac, "This is (I hope) the toughest battle I'll ever have to face in my life, and I've got to feel that I'm fighting it with my own hands and my own money. . . . So I ask you, Deac, to take me off the payroll."

Deac wrote back, "I understand—and you win."

Jerry checked into a mental hospital for six weeks. When she came home, Ernie cooked and cleaned and waited on her. She got better, and he got restless. "I'm afraid being in England has spoiled me for the duration," he wrote to a friend. "I've got to be doing something a little exciting or I go nuts."

By fall, Jerry was healthy enough for Ernie to think about working again. He suggested to Scripps Howard that he take a three-month trip to the Orient in December. He wanted to write about places like the Philippines, Hong Kong, Burma, Singapore, and the East Indies. "I feel it important that we should kick the column off again with something big," he told Deac Parker. The trip was approved, and Ernie began making preparations to leave.

But on December 7, something happened that changed Ernie's plans. The Japanese bombed Pearl Harbor, in Hawaii. Nearly four thousand Americans were killed or wounded. Over half of the American navy's fleet was destroyed or severely damaged. The following day, the United States declared war against Japan. Three days later, Japan's allies, Germany and Italy, declared war on the United States. The war in Europe had become World War II. Ernie's trip to the Orient would have to wait. Instead, he climbed into his car and drove up the West Coast in search of new material for the column.

The short break hadn't hurt his popularity with his readers. Forty-seven newspapers were printing his columns. But Ernie was so lonely and depressed he could hardly work. Within weeks after leaving Albuquerque, letters and phone calls from Jerry and their friends revealed that once again she was not doing well.

As always, Ernie's response was to keep working. "I've got to get back to the columns with a vim and restore an interest in life and in myself," he wrote her. "I've got to work hard again, and brood less, and enjoy things more, and drink less."

His worries about Jerry, combined with the demands of producing a daily column, were getting Ernie down. He was desperate for a solution to her problems but could find none. Realizing that nothing could return them to happier times, Ernie and Jerry decided to end their marriage. They were divorced on April 14, 1942.

Ernie hoped that the divorce would not be permanent. He thought that maybe such a drastic move would shock Jerry into getting better. If that didn't happen, Ernie felt sure that she would have to be committed to a mental hospital.

Ernie didn't know where to go from there. Scripps Howard wanted him to return to England to write about the training of American troops there. He was so low he couldn't even think about writing, but doing nothing had never been Ernie's style either. He decided he would go overseas for a few months, then resume his travel column.

Just before leaving New York, Ernie wrote to Jerry, "Be my old Jerry when I come back. I love you."

HOTEL ALGONQUIN
NEW YORK

June 18 -42
12 M

Tuesday Night

Darling -
I am taking off within the hour. I came here because I couldn't stand to go to the Piccadilly without you. I am not excited about going, but do feel a last-minute sense of fatalism or something. I am all alone. Be my old Jerry when I come back, I love you.

Ernie

CHAPTER
7

Alongside the GIs

In June of 1942, Ernie arrived in Ireland to spend some time in the training camps before continuing on to England. His spirits were so low it took him "about two hours every morning to get the spark of life burning again."

But the soldiers he met took to him right away, and his mood lifted a little. Many of them had read his columns back home. To them, Ernie was a celebrity. But they were surprised to find that he was just a regular guy doing the same things they were doing. He didn't even look like anybody special. He was just a puny little man in baggy clothes and a stocking cap. Ernie resisted wearing an officer's uniform like the other correspondents. "An officer's uniform would scare them and put them on guard, and I couldn't lie around half the night shooting the bull with them," he told Lee.

It was important to Ernie that he live with the soldiers—eat with them, sleep with them, even run obstacle courses with them. He figured folks back in the States would want to know what everyday life was like for their sons, husbands, brothers, and boyfriends. He was right. "Every new arrival over here reports that the column is just what the people want to know and nobody else is doing it," he wrote to Jerry.

There were rumors around the training camps that the troops would see some action soon. If the rumors were true, Ernie wanted to go with them. His chance came with Operation Torch, the military code name for the invasion of German-occupied North Africa by the British and American Allied forces.

On November 22, 1942, two weeks after Allied troops invaded Africa, Ernie and a group of other correspondents arrived in Oran, Algeria, on the coast of the Mediterranean Sea. He walked down the gangplank of a British transport ship "feeling self-conscious and ridiculous and old in Army uniform" (which he was now required to wear) and an armband with a big letter *C* for "correspondent." He took with him a duffel bag, a bedroll, a knapsack, a gas mask, a helmet, a canteen, a typewriter, and "one of the Ten Best Colds of 1942."

It seemed as if he had brought along everything he needed but a good dose of self-confidence. He complained to Lee that his first columns were "confused and inadequate." But if he had lost confidence in his work, he hadn't lost his gift for writing. The folks at home thought his columns were fascinating.

Despite the excitement of being with the troops in North Africa, Ernie's despair over Jerry and the divorce

still weighed heavily on him. He regretted ever divorcing her. She was sick and often made his life miserable, but he still loved her. On Thanksgiving night, a sad and lonely Ernie wrote Jerry and suggested that they consider getting married again. "It wouldn't bring me home any quicker," he wrote, "but somehow I'd feel happier about things." He asked an Army judge to draw up the legal papers needed for a marriage by proxy, which meant that a marriage could be performed without Ernie being present. He sent the papers to Jerry's nurse and asked that they be given to Jerry when she was better. Now all he could do was wait—and work.

In January 1943, Ernie went to an army airfield in Biskra, an Algerian town near the border of Tunisia. He planned to write several columns about bomber pilots and their crews before returning home to America to resume his travel column. But Ernie's next adventure would change those plans—and Ernie—forever. From the airfield he headed for the mountains of Tunisia, where he got his first glimpse at the front lines (where fighting is heaviest in a battle). There he met members of the infantry, soldiers trained to fight on foot—not from an airplane or a ship, but right there on the ground. From the beginning of his war coverage, he had felt a kinship with all the men he met. But his affection for the infantryman was different. In the GI (as infantrymen were called), Ernie found the ultimate hero. "They are the mud-rain-frost-and-wind boys. . . . And in the end they are the guys that wars can't be won without," he explained.

Unlike the other war correspondents in North Africa at

that time, Ernie did not want to stay near military head-quarters and receive instructions on where to go and what to write about. Not Ernie. He was right there in the trenches with the GIs. He slept in chicken houses, under wagons, in cactus patches, in trees, and on the stone floors of vacant buildings. He was free to roam about, going wherever he pleased and writing whatever he wanted.

He got to know generals and other important military leaders, but he preferred being with the enlisted men (men of low rank, not officers). His friendly, homespun ways made him a welcome sight in the camps, pup tents, and makeshift mess halls, where he and the soldiers often chatted like lifelong buddies. When Ernie sat down at his typewriter to catch up on his columns, a crowd of curious soldiers often gathered to look over his shoulder and admire the speed of his two-fingered typing.

While other correspondents wrote about military strategy, major battles, or the political aspects of the war, Ernie wrote about the details of soldier life. He described how the men cooked their meals in gasoline cans and washed their mess kits (dishes and cookware) with sand and toilet paper. He explained how to dig a slit trench in the desert. And as he had done in the travel columns, Ernie often wrote about himself and his experiences. No detail was too trivial for Ernie. "For a lifetime . . . I thought the world would come to an end unless I changed my socks every day," he wrote. "Now . . . I go two weeks at a time without even taking [them] off."

When folks back home opened their morning papers to

Ernie's column, they didn't read about nameless, faceless fighting men. They read about Sergeant Gibson Fryer, of Troy, Alabama, who had a picture of his wife on the handle of his gun. They learned that Ernie had marched through the mud behind Sergeant Vincent Conners, of Imogene, Iowa. And they laughed about Master Sergeant Woodrow Daniel, from Jacksonville, Florida, who got a bottle of Coke in a package from home. Ernie's soldiers had nicknames and hometowns, sweethearts and mothers, funny habits and interesting hobbies. They were young boys from towns and cities across America, places where Ernie's old Ford coupe had probably taken him during his years on the road.

Mothers clipped Ernie's columns and sent them to their sons overseas. The columns also appeared daily in *Stars and Stripes,* the military newspaper. The soldiers got a kick out of reading about themselves and their buddies. Ernie was describing the war through a soldier's eyes and with a soldier's voice. Somehow, that made them feel better—less alone and more appreciated. Years later, General Omar Bradley told Ernie's Aunt Mary that his men "always fought better when Ernie was around."

Trudging along muddy mountain paths in the dark and sleeping on the cold ground, Ernie had become an expert on the hardships of life in the infantry. Dinner was cold rations from a can, and bathing meant washing his feet in his helmet once a week. Ernie had given up all "the little things that made life normal back home"—including alcohol, which was hard to come by in North Africa. For a forty-two-year-old prone to sickness, the cold desert and

Ernie had a bad habit of forgetting to wear his helmet. But it did come in handy as a tub for washing his feet (above).

Although Ernie spent most of his time with the infantry (right), he also found time to visit with other members of the war team, including this evacuation hospital in Italy (below).

irregular sleep schedule should have sapped his energy. Yet surprisingly, Ernie found himself healthy and feeling the best he had felt in years.

Besides renewed health, Ernie had another reason to feel happy: his urge to keep moving had left him. He was beginning to put down some roots among the tired, dirty soldiers he wrote about. If Ernie ever felt a sense of belonging, it was right here, shoulder to shoulder with GI Joe. For the first time in his life, Ernie felt a connection to something. As the months slipped by, Ernie gave up the idea of returning to America to travel. He decided to stick with his war coverage. Ernie Pyle had found his place.

In February, Ernie got a letter from Jerry. It had been some time since he had sent his marriage proposal. Bundled up in heavy underwear, two sweaters, and coveralls, he sat down on a tree stump in the cold wind to read it. His excitement quickly turned to disappointment. Jerry had turned him down.

But less than one month later, on March 12, 1943, Ernie got some unexpected news in a cable from a London news bureau: "New York reports you married former wife by proxy."

Ernie immediately cabled Jerry, "Just received word marriage from London. So happy could bust. Love you."

When he finally had a chance to sit down and write, he told her, "I think one of the reasons I wanted this is that if anything should happen to me before this war is over, I wanted to go out that way—as we were. . . . Now I feel some peace with the world again."

CHAPTER
8

The Most Prayed-For Man with the Troops

By 1943, Ernie was the most popular war correspondent in America. His columns were carried in about eighty newspapers. Fan letters poured in by the hundreds. A publisher, Henry Holt and Company, was preparing a book of Ernie's North African columns, to be called *Here is Your War.*

With all his fame, his bank account was surely growing larger. But Ernie had little use for money, especially in a foxhole. He wrote to Lee, "You just pile up the money for me, Doctor, and after awhile we'll go fishin'."

The longer Ernie stayed at the front in Tunisia, the more he saw of the hard and sad realities of war. The beautiful African hills were "gradually turning red with blood." Sometimes Ernie feared he was getting too used to seeing death and destruction, yet other times he was deeply affected by the cruelty of war. "I find I can look on rows of fresh graves without a lump in my throat," he wrote. "And there are times when I feel that I can't stand it and will have to leave."

In May 1943, German and Italian forces in North Africa surrendered to Great Britain and the U.S. But the war in Europe was far from over. The Allied forces had begun preparations for Operation Huskey, the invasion of the Italian island of Sicily. From there they planned to invade mainland Italy, hoping to force Italy to surrender so that Germany would have to fend for itself.

Lee Miller suggested that Ernie return home for a rest. But Ernie wanted to stay a while to cover Operation Huskey. While he waited for the troops to move, Ernie stayed with the other correspondents at a press camp in Algiers. There he wrote the final chapter of *Here is Your War*. That piece was one of Ernie's most soul-searching and emotionally revealing works.

"It may be that the war has changed me," he wrote. "I know that I find more and more that I wish to be alone." After experiencing the horrors of war, Ernie questioned "how any survivor of war can ever be cruel to anything, ever again." And he expressed his respect and affection for the thousands of soldiers who had died in the war, many of whom he had talked to, slept beside, laughed with, and written about. "When we leave here for the next shore," he wrote, "there is nothing we can do for the ones beneath the wooden crosses, except perhaps to pause and murmur, 'Thanks, pal.'"

After covering the Sicilian campaign, which lasted five weeks, Ernie was finally ready to go home for a vacation. He knew that the war would go on for months and possibly years. He still had a lot of writing ahead of him. He felt guilty for leaving when the soldiers had to stay, but tired and homesick, Ernie needed to "refreshen [his] sagging brain and drooping frame."

In September, Lee Miller met Ernie in New York City, and the two of them checked into the Algonquin Hotel. Almost immediately, the telephone began ringing nonstop. Everyone wanted to see and talk to Ernie Pyle. Newspaper reporters and radio stations wanted interviews. Photographers wanted pictures. A Hollywood producer wanted to discuss making a movie about Ernie. Letters and telegrams arrived by the sackful.

Ernie was overwhelmed. His first column from the U.S. was titled "Fed Up and Bogged Down." "How should a war correspondent who has been away a long time begin his first column after he returns to his homeland?" he wrote. "Frankly, I don't know. I can't truthfully say,

Ernie agreed to do only one radio broadcast during his visit home in 1943—an advertisement for war bonds. He was interviewed by Secretary of the Treasury Henry Morgenthau Jr.

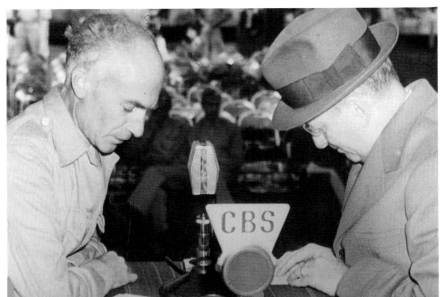

'My, it's wonderful to be back,' because I haven't had a moment to sense whether it's wonderful or not. In my first forty-eight hours in America I got two hours' sleep, said 'no' three hundred twenty-four times, lost my pocketbook and caught a bad cold."

After a hectic week, Ernie finally got to Albuquerque to see Jerry. His excitement over seeing her again quickly turned to disappointment. He knew right away that she was in terrible shape. The months and years of being alone, trying to cope with her illness, had all but destroyed her. None of her attempts to kick her addictions to drugs and alcohol had worked. "I can hardly look at her," he wrote to a friend, "without kind of crying inside at her awful tragedy—and mine."

By November, his vacation nearly over, Ernie's thoughts returned to the war in Europe. "I've never hated to do anything as badly in my life as I hate to go back to the front," he wrote in a column. "I dread it and I'm afraid of it." But he belonged there in the trenches with the soldiers. They needed a voice, and Ernie Pyle was the best one they had.

When forty-three-year-old Ernie left Albuquerque in December 1943, he left behind the warm weather, a comfortable bed, and all hope of renewed happiness with Jerry. He was greeted in Italy by bitter cold, knee-deep mud, freezing rain, and "the old familiar crash and thunder of the big guns in [his] reluctant ears."

Ernie set up a routine right away. He would spend several days at the front, then return to the press camp for about five days to write. The other correspondents often gathered in Ernie's tent to talk, drink, and play gin rummy.

As usual, Ernie struggled with doubts about his work and feared he was writing "the same old stuff." Don Whitehead, a correspondent for the Associated Press and a close friend of Ernie's, remembered one night when Ernie complained to him that his writing was no good. Ernie handed over a few of his columns and asked what he thought of them. The first one Don read was to become one of Ernie's most well-known columns: "The Death of Captain Waskow." Henry T. Waskow, of Belton, Texas, was an infantry commander killed in the mountains of Italy. Ernie described the night his body was carried down the mountain on the back of a mule and how his men reacted to his death. "This was the kind of writing all of us were striving for," Don recalled, "the picture we were trying to paint in words for the people at home." After reading the column, Don turned to Ernie and said, "If this is a sample from a guy who has lost his touch, then the rest of us had better go home."

Ernie may have had doubts about his talents, but the rest of America did not. The reaction to the Waskow piece was sensational. The *Washington Daily News* devoted its entire front page to the piece. The paper sold out that day.

The Captain Waskow column put the final seal of approval on Ernie's status as the top war correspondent in the country. The *Saturday Evening Post* called him "the most prayed-for man with the American troops." His column now appeared in over two hundred newspapers and was read by some thirteen million Americans each day.

Index

EDITORIALS ... 30
Columnists ... 30–33
Comics ... 23
Mrs. Roosevelt ... 24
9 to 6 30 ... 18
Thinking ... 28, 27
Pictures ... 18, 19
Society ... 25
Sports ... 2v, 30
Radio ... 24
Woman's ... 24
Pears ... 24, 25

23d Year—No. 52

The Washington Daily News

Entered as Second Class Matter at D. C. Post Office

2 CENTS

MONDAY, JANUARY 10, 1944

Weather

Fair; lowest tem-
perature near 22
degrees.   Tuesday
fair and warmer.
Today at 8:30 a.
m. 23, 9 30 a. m.
24, 10 30 a. m. 27,
noon, 32 .1 p. m.,
34.

Final Home Edition

Page One is different today because we t h o u g h t Ernie Pyle's story would tell you more about the war than headlines that Russians are 35 miles inside Poland, or that Yank fliers are backing up Yugoslavs.

By ERNIE PYLE

AT THE FRONT LINES IN ITALY, Jan. 10 (By Wireless)—In this war I have known a lot of officers who were loved and respected by the soldiers under them. But never have I crossed the trail of any man as beloved as Capt. Henry T. Waskow of Belton, Tex.

Capt. Waskow was a company commander in the 36th Division. He had been in this company since long before he left the States. He was very young, only in his middle twenties, but he carried in him a sincerity and gentleness that made people want to be guided by him.

"After my own father, he comes next," a sergeant told me.

"He always looked after us," a soldier said. "He'd go to bat for us every time."

"I've never known him to do anything unkind," another one said.

* * *

I WAS at the foot of the mule trail the night they brought Capt. Waskow down. The moon was nearly full, and you could see far up the trail, and even part way across the valley. Soldiers made shadows as they walked.

Dead men had been coming down the mountain all evening, lashed onto the backs of mules. They came lying belly down across the wooden packsaddle, their heads hanging down on the left side of the mule, their stiffened legs sticking awkwardly from the other side, bobbing up and down as the mule walked.

The Italian mule skinners were afraid to walk beside dead men, so Americans had to lead the mules down that night. Even the Americans were reluctant to unlash and lift off the bodies, when they got to the bottom, so an officer had to do it himself and ask others to help.

The first one came early in the morning. They slid him down from the mule, and stood him on his feet for a moment. In the half light he might have been merely a sick man standing there leaning on the other. Then they laid him on the ground in the shadow of the stone wall alongside the road.

I don't know who that first one was. You feel small in the presence of dead men, and you don't ask silly questions . . . .

We left him there beside the road, that first one, and we all went back into the cowshed and sat on watercans or lay on the straw, waiting for the next batch of mules.

Somebody said the dead soldier had been dead for four days, and then nobody said anything more about him. We talked for an hour or more; the dead man lay all alone, outside in the shadow of the wall.

* * *

THEN a soldier came into the cowshed and said there were some more bodies outside. We went out into the road. Four mules stood there in the moonlight, in the road where the trail came down off the mountain. The soldiers who led them stood there waiting.

"This one is Capt. Waskow," one of them said quickly.

Two men unlashed his body from the mule and lifted it off and laid it in the shadow beside the stone wall. Other men took the other bodies off. Finally, there were five lying end to end in a long row. You don't cover up dead men in the combat zones. They just lie there in the shadows until somebody else comes after them.

The uncertain mules moved off to their olive groves. The men in the road seemed reluctant to leave. They stood around, and gradually I could sense them moving, one by one, close to Capt. Waskow's body. Not so much to look, I think, as to say something in finality to him and to themselves. I stood close by and I could hear.

One soldier came and looked down, and he said out loud:

"God damn it!"

Another one came, and he said, "God damn it to hell anyway!" He looked down for a few last moments and then turned and left.

Another man came. I think he was an officer. It was hard to tell officers from men in the dim light, for everybody was grimy and dirty. The man looked down into the dead captain's face and then spoke directly to him, as tho he were alive:

"I'm sorry, old man."

Then a soldier came and stood beside the officer and bent over, and he too spoke to his dead captain, not in a whisper but awfully tender, and he said:

"I sure am sorry, sir." '

Then the first man squatted down, and he reached down and took the Captain's hand, and he sat there for a full five minutes holding the dead hand in his own and looking intently into the d e a d face. And he never uttered a sound all the time he sat there.

Finally he put the hand down. He reached up and gently straightened the points of t h e Captain's shirt collar, and then he sort of rearranged the tattered edges of his uniform around the wound, and then he got up and walked away down the road in the moonlight, all alone.

The rest of us went back into the cowshed, leaving the five dead men lying in a line, end to end, in the shadow of the low stone wall. We lay down on the straw in the cowshed, and pretty soon we were all asleep.

The front page of the *Washington Daily News*, January 10, 1944

On the front lines in Italy, however, Ernie was more concerned with his survival than his popularity back home. The winter was bitter cold, and he was getting all too used to diving for cover from flying bullets and exploding shells. "There are certain moments when a plain old ditch can be dearer to you than any possession on earth," Ernie wrote. Exhausted, cold, and hungry, he and the GIs trudged through snow with heavy equipment and dug foxholes in the frozen ground.

Even when he managed to find a place to work with a roof over his head, Ernie was rarely out of danger. Once, after he had set up temporary quarters with other correspondents in an abandoned villa in Nettuno, Italy, the villa was bombed. No one was seriously hurt, but it left Ernie's typewriter covered with dust and mortar, his boots filled to the toes with broken glass, and his nerves more than a little frayed.

As always, Ernie kept Jerry posted on his adventures, his health, and his love and concern for her. "Your being well again is the only thing that really means anything in my life," he told her, and offered to come home if she needed him. But Jerry must have known that Ernie was exactly where he really wanted to be. Although she worried about his safety, she didn't pressure him to quit. Ernie had made it clear that his commitment to GI Joe came first. If Jerry resented that, she didn't say.

On April 5, 1944, Ernie left Italy and headed for London. Nearly 160,000 Allied soldiers waited in England, preparing to cross the English Channel to free German-occupied France. Ernie waited with them. He was one of twenty-eight correspondents chosen to go along on the first phase of the invasion. Although Ernie loved London, being in a big city made him nervous and restless. He realized he preferred to be with the soldiers in the field. His mood lightened when he got the exciting news that he had won the 1943 Pulitzer prize for "distinguished correspondence." Ernie was so surprised and proud he "damn near started to cry."

Two long, tense months went by. No one knew exactly when the invasion would take place. The weather had to be perfect. The tide had to be just right. Finally, on June 6, 1944, over five thousand ships left England carrying the Allied troops to the beaches of Normandy, France. More than 2,500 Allied soldiers died storming the beach that day, which would be known forever as D day. The

Ernie's work was bringing him acclaim: the *Detroit Free Press* reported that he was the best correspondent the war had seen, and he was awarded the 1943 Pulitzer prize. Yet the pain of the Normandy invasion (below) forced him to flee Europe.

next day, Ernie walked along Omaha Beach. "The wreckage was vast and startling," he wrote. Burned jeeps, tangled rolls of telephone wire, and empty life rafts littered the beach. Scattered along the water's edge were socks, sewing kits, Bibles, hand grenades, water-soaked cigarettes, and photographs of soldiers' loved ones back home. And everywhere there were dead bodies. Ernie wrote two columns about what he saw that terrible day: "The Horrible Waste of War" and "A Long Thin Line of Personal Anguish."

While the war against Hitler continued in western Europe, Japan had been taking control of islands in the Pacific Ocean, including Guam, Singapore, Indonesia, and the Philippines. Ernie had done such a fine job of boosting the morale of the troops in Europe that the armed forces in the Pacific wanted him to spend some time there. Ernie agreed to go, but only after a rest at home. That September in Paris, he wrote his last column from the European front. "By the time you read this," it said, "the old man will be on his way back to America. . . . I'm leaving for one reason only—because I have just got to stop. . . . My spirit is wobbly and my mind is confused. The hurt has finally become too great." With that, Ernie said "goodbye—and good luck" to the soldiers in Europe.

CHAPTER
9

To the Pacific

Ernie arrived in the United States on September 18, 1944, sneezing and sniffling and just plain worn out. Waiting to meet him at the airport in Albuquerque were Jerry, her nurse, Ella Streger, and Ernie's old buddy Paige. After the foxholes and bedrolls Ernie had called home for the last year, his little house was a welcome sight. More than anything, Ernie just wanted some peace and quiet. But even more than on his last visit home, he was flooded with visitors and phone calls. Later Ernie wrote a column titled "Hardly a Vacation," in which he described the ups and downs of his fame. "Sometimes I feel like sitting down and crying because my old life is gone," he wrote.

Everyone wanted something from Ernie: an interview, an autograph, his presence at a dinner party, information about a loved one overseas. Ernie politely turned away most of the requests, but he did agree to one: receiving an honorary doctorate degree from the University of New Mexico in Albuquerque. When Ernie had left college twenty-one years earlier, he never dreamed he would some day receive a degree that listed so many accomplishments. It read: "Ernest Taylor Pyle, writer, journalist, war correspondent, world traveler, and interpreter of the American way of life, sympathetic and understanding friend of our soldiers on the fields of battle, friend and comforter of thousands of relatives whose loved ones have fallen in the service of their country." He was forty-four years old.

Ernie's busy schedule left little time to spend alone with Jerry. The house was constantly crowded with visitors, as well as Jerry's nurse and the two secretaries hired to handle Ernie's mail and phone calls. When Ernie first arrived home, he thought Jerry seemed to be doing better. But within a week or two, he realized she was very ill. She sat for hours on the edge of her bed, staring into space, not talking. A doctor came by every day to check

Jerry's illness and the stress it caused Ernie are both visible in this photo with their dog, Cheetah.

on her. One day he told Ernie, "I might as well tell you, we're in for a rough time ahead."

He was right. The next day Jerry made another attempt at suicide. She was taken to a sanitarium to recover. Ernie was devastated. "What to do now?" he wrote to Lee. "I've long ago given up hope for [her], yet there's nothing to do but hope."

After a month of treatment, Jerry had made enough progress to go to California with Ernie to visit the Cavanaughs and to see the set of *The Story of GI Joe,* the movie being made about Ernie. About the same time, another book of Ernie's war columns was published. Titled *Brave Men,* the book's dedication read: "In Solemn Salute To Those Thousands of Our Comrades—Great, Brave Men That They Were—For Whom There Will Be No Homecoming, Ever."

In late December 1944, Ernie and Jerry said good-bye at a railway station in Los Angeles, California. Jerry was returning to Albuquerque with her nurse while Ernie prepared for his trip to the Pacific. Fearing for his safety, Jerry had begged him not to go, but Ernie felt it was something he had to do. As they parted, Ernie handed her a note that read, "My darling: I love you terribly, and always have and always will."

Ernie arrived in Oahu, Hawaii, on a warm January day in 1945. By then, American forces had fought to free many of the South Pacific islands captured by Japan. The Allied forces planned to take the Japanese islands of Iwo Jima and Okinawa, then invade the mainland.

From Oahu, Ernie flew to several islands to cover the

Falling in with the Marines in the Pacific. Ernie is easy to spot since correspondents were not allowed to carry weapons.

various branches of the armed forces fighting on the Pacific front. He was still tired and troubled from his trip home and found it hard to get back into the routine of writing. His biggest obstacle was that he just couldn't seem to connect with the troops in the Pacific the way he had with the infantry in Europe. He liked the sailors he talked to, but he thought they complained too much about how hard things were for them and how much they wanted to go home. Ernie felt they were having an easier time of it than the boys in Europe, and he didn't keep his feelings to himself. In columns with titles like "Their Lives Are Pretty Good" and "Europe This Is Not," he wrote, "The boys ask you a thousand times how this compares with the other side. I can only answer that this is much better. . . . I've heard some boys say, 'I'd trade this for a foxhole any day.' You just have to keep your mouth shut to a remark like that."

In March, Ernie boarded the aircraft carrier USS *Cabot*, part of a convoy setting out for Iwo Jima with planes and artillery. The trip was not a happy one for Ernie. He was beginning to worry that his luck was running out. "I feel that I've used up all my chances," he told a reporter. "And I hate it. . . . I don't want to be killed."

Ernie spent three weeks on the *Cabot*. By then, word was circulating that there would be an invasion of Okinawa. Operation Iceberg, as it was called, was scheduled to begin on Easter Sunday, April 1, 1945. Ernie thought he should go along, but he was scared of making another landing. After three nights of tossing and turning and worrying, Ernie made up his mind. He would go. He wanted to cover the Marines, a branch of the service he had never written about. While he waited for the operation to begin, Ernie was comforted by a warm and loving letter from Jerry. "My love reaches out to you—so strongly— and wants so much for you—Bless you my Ernie."

Before daybreak on Easter morning, Ernie ate ham and eggs for breakfast, then waited for his turn to leave the *Cabot*. War correspondents were not allowed to go ashore until at least the fifth wave of troops. Ernie was on the seventh. While he waited, he watched the invasion through binoculars. "There's nothing romantic whatever in knowing that an hour from now you may be dead," he wrote.

Finally, at about ten o'clock, Ernie went ashore. He had dreaded "the sight of the beach littered with mangled bodies" as he had seen at Normandy. But Ernie was surprised to find that on the section of beach where he landed, there were no bodies. The invasion had been nothing like what he had expected. (By the time the invasion ended more than two months later, however, nearly 50,000 Americans had been killed or wounded.)

"What a wonderful feeling!" he wrote. Ernie felt like a new man.

After six days on land, he boarded the command ship USS *Panamint* to write his columns about the invasion and to rest. He also wrote Jerry. "Everything is fine with me now. You can't know the relief I felt, for I had dreaded this one terribly."

Just days later, word came that there was to be another invasion. On April 16, the 77th Infantry Division was to seize the little Japanese island of Ie Shima. Ernie decided to go ashore, but not right away. He had promised himself he would not go on another landing on the first day of an invasion.

On the second day of the invasion, Ernie went ashore with some other correspondents. Because of the danger of stepping on a land mine, a guide escorted them to a command post. When Ernie got to the post, he felt at home again. The infantry was there, and Ernie felt friendly and relaxed. After spending the afternoon chatting with the soldiers, he decided to sleep on the island that night rather than return to the ship. The next day, April 18, Ernie climbed into a jeep with four Marines bound for a command post on the other side of the island. The road was narrow but well traveled and cleared of mines. As the group approached the city of Ie, the dreaded sound of machine-gun fire pierced the air. Dust flew as bullets hit the road. Ernie and the others dove from the jeep into the shelter of a roadside ditch.

Ernie lay flat on the ground, waiting. Then he raised his head to look for the others. When he saw one of his

Ernie's coffin was set in a long row of graves. Since the fighting was close by, those attending the funeral had to wear helmets and carry weapons.

companions, he smiled and asked, "Are you all right?" That instant, gunfire came again—and Ernie was killed.

News of Ernie Pyle's death stunned and saddened the nation. In his public announcement of Ernie's death, President Truman said, "No man in this war has so well told the story of the American fighting man as American fighting men wanted it told. He deserves the gratitude of all his countrymen."

Soldiers killed in action were usually buried without coffins. But out of love and respect for Ernie, one soldier used packing crates to build Ernie a flimsy coffin that was placed in a long row of graves on the shore of Ie Shima.

On the spot by the roadside where Ernie had died, the soldiers erected a wooden sign that read:

AT THIS SPOT
THE 77TH INFANTRY DIVISION
LOST A BUDDY
ERNIE PYLE
18 APRIL 1945

Afterword

Ernie once wrote that he hoped he lasted "until the sun shines in the world again." Sadly, he did not. But only three weeks after his death, on May 8, 1945, Germany surrendered. In hopeful anticipation of that day, Ernie had prepared a column to be released at that time. It was in his pocket on the day he died.

Titled "On Victory in Europe," the piece expressed Ernie's affection for the troops there. "My heart is still in Europe," he wrote, "and that's why I am writing this column. It is to the boys who were my friends for so long. My one regret of the war is that I was not with them when it ended."

On August 14, 1945, Japan surrendered. World War II was over.

When the war-weary soldiers returned to their families and loved ones across America, they were received with welcome arms. And they had Ernie to thank—at least in part—for the respect and understanding that greeted them. "Thousands of our men will soon be returning to you," Ernie had written. "They have been gone a long time and they have seen and done and felt things you cannot know. They will be changed."

To the end of the war and beyond, Ernie Pyle was the soldier's voice.

Notes

page 37

Ernie often wrote "we" in columns, but he was usually alone.

page 49

Although Ernie was eligible to be drafted into the army, the draft board allowed him to leave the U.S. for six months in 1942 to visit London.

page 52

When Ernie's six month leave was up, he asked Lee Miller to apply for an extension. Shortly thereafter, the army stopped drafting men over the age of thirty-eight. Ernie was forty-two, so he no longer needed permission to be out of the country.

Although women served in all branches of the armed forces during World War II, they did not fight in combat. Therefore, the subjects of Ernie's war columns were almost exclusively men.

page 68

Jerry refused to wear a wedding ring until 1945, twenty years after she and Ernie were married. Ernie sent her the ring from San Francisco—at her request—before he left for the Pacific.

page 71

Besides some farmhouses, there wasn't much to be found on the tiny island of Ie Shima except two Japanese airstrips. American troops took the airstrips and most of the island with little effort and few casualties. But the Japanese were determined to keep their island. Ie Shima was hilly and covered with caves and brush, good hiding places for Japanese soldiers, who came out at night to attack the Americans or to plant land mines. In six days of fighting, about two hundred Americans and nearly five thousand Japanese were killed.

page 72

Although newspaper headlines told the country "That Girl Takes News Bravely," Jerry's health declined rapidly in the months following Ernie's death. After coming down with the flu, she was hospitalized and died on November 23, 1945.

Bibliography

"Dana Boy Makes Good." *Time* 43, no. 24 (June 12, 1944): 64.

"Ernie Pyle's War." *Time* 44, no. 3 (July 17, 1944): 65-66.

"Ernie Was Tired." *Newsweek* 24, no. 12 (September 18, 1944): 88.

Duffield, Marcus. "Ernie Pyle in Africa." *The Nation* 157, no. 21 (November 20, 1943): 589-590.

Faircloth, Rudy. *Typewriter Soldier.* Tabor City, North Carolina: Atlantic, 1982.

Gilbert, Martin. *The Second World War: A Complete History.* New York: Henry Holt, 1989.

Graff, Stewart. *The Story of World War II.* New York: Dutton, 1978.

Hovey, Graham B. "This Is Ernie Pyle's War." *The New Republic* 3, no. 24 (December 11, 1944): 804-806.

Keegan, John. *The Second World War.* New York: Viking, 1989.

Leckie, Robert. *Delivered from Evil: The Saga of World War II.* New York: Harper and Row, 1987.

Miller, Lee G. *An Ernie Pyle Album: Indiana to Ie Shima.* New York: William Sloane Associates, 1946.

——*The Story of Ernie Pyle.* New York: Viking, 1950.

Nichols, David, ed. *Ernie's America: The Best of Ernie Pyle's 1930s Travel Dispatches.* New York: Random House, 1989.

——*Ernie's War: The Best of Ernie Pyle's World War II Dispatches.* New York: Random House, 1986.

Pyle, Ernie. *Brave Men.* New York: Henry Holt, 1944.

——*Last Chapter.* New York: Henry Holt, 1946.

Sutton, Felix. *The How and Why Wonder Book of World War II.* New York: Grosset and Dunlap, 1962.

All quotations in this book were taken from the above sources.

Index

All illustrations are reproduced courtesy of the Ernie Pyle State Historical Site, except: front cover, p. 2, UPI/Bettmann; back cover (W & C 1349), pp. 44 background (W & C 1103), 64 (W & C 1041), 79 (III-SC 191705), National Archives; p. 17, Indiana University Archives; p. 42, the Museum of New Mexico, #138706; p. 49, Manuscripts Department, Lilly Library, Indiana University, Bloomington, IN. Every effort has been made to secure permission for the photos on pp. 7, 11, and 21. Any corrections in this regard will be made at the earliest opportunity.

12/96

E.R. Libby Memorial Library